OXFORD
First Book
of
Children
of the
World

OXFORD
First Book
of
Children
of the
World

OXFORD

UNIVERSITY PRESS

OXFORD
UNIVERSITY PRESS

Great Clarendon Street, Oxford OX2 6DP

Oxford University Press is a department of the University of Oxford.
It furthers the University's objective of excellence in research, scholarship,
and education by publishing worldwide in

Oxford New York

Athens Auckland Bangkok Bogotá Buenos Aires Calcutta
Cape Town Chennai Dar es Salaam Delhi Florence Hong Kong Istanbul
Karachi Kuala Lumpur Madrid Melbourne Mexico City Mumbai
Nairobi Paris São Paulo Singapore Taipei Tokyo Toronto Warsaw

with associated companies in Berlin Ibadan

Oxford is a registered trade mark of Oxford University Press
in the UK and in certain other countries

© Rebecca Treays 2000
The moral rights of the author have been asserted

First published 2000

British Library Cataloguing in Publication Data available

ISBN 0-19-910698-3 (hardback)
ISBN 0-19-910770-X (paperback)

1 3 5 7 9 10 8 6 4 2

Designed by White Design
Printed in Hong Kong

Contents

Introduction

In this book you will meet children from all over the world. You will learn about their families, their homes, their schools, and their likes and dislikes. You will find out about life in other countries, and discover the differences and similarities in children's lives everywhere.

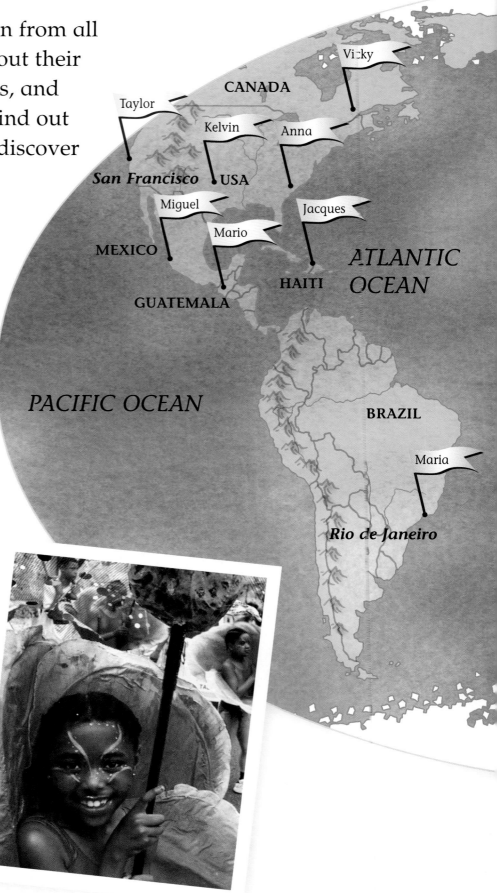

▲ My name is Mario. I live in a country called Guatemala. My town is in a valley in the mountains.

▶ My name is Maria. I live in Brazil in a big city called Rio de Janeiro. It is on the coast and has a brilliant beach called the Cococabana.

My name is Kristin. I live in a fishing village in Norway. It is often snowy here. I learned to ski almost before I could walk!

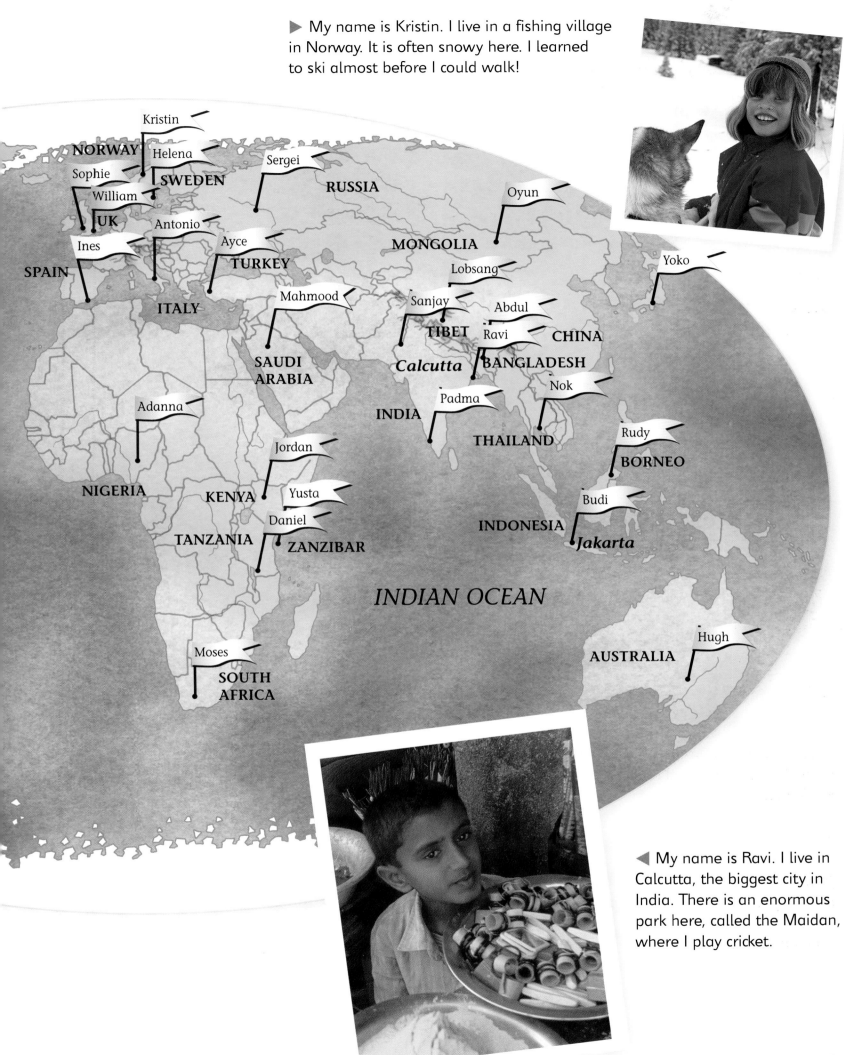

Kristin

NORWAY

Helena

SWEDEN

Sophie

William

UK

Antonio

Ines

SPAIN

ITALY

Ayce

TURKEY

Sergei

RUSSIA

Mahmood

SAUDI
ARABIA

Oyun

MONGOLIA

Lobsang

Sanjay

TIBET

Calcutta

Ravi

Abdul

CHINA

Yoko

BANGLADESH

Nok

Padma

INDIA

THAILAND

Rudy

BORNEO

Adanna

NIGERIA

Jordan

KENYA

Yusta

Daniel

TANZANIA

ZANZIBAR

Budi

INDONESIA

Jakarta

INDIAN OCEAN

Moses

SOUTH
AFRICA

Hugh

AUSTRALIA

My name is Ravi. I live in Calcutta, the biggest city in India. There is an enormous park here, called the Maidan, where I play cricket.

Our Families

Children all over the world live in families. But there are many different kinds. Some children live with just one parent. Others live with two parents, brothers, sisters, grandparents, uncles, aunts and cousins! Whatever their size, families help each other. They share household jobs, money and food so that everyone is looked after.

Ayce

My name is Ayce. I live in Turkey with my mum, dad, three sisters, two uncles, two aunts, eight cousins, and one grandmother. There are nineteen of us altogether. It's fun because there is always someone to play with. My mum and dad both go out to work, so during the day my aunties look after me and my sisters.

◀ This photo was taken on my grandmother's sixtieth birthday. I am sitting on the bottom step, wearing a flowery skirt.

Vicky

My name is Vicky. I live with my mum, dad and brother in Canada. I'm eight and my brother is ten. He's usually quite nice to me, but he gets cross when I borrow his computer games. I have got some cousins but they live a long way away. We only see them once a year when we all go to my grandma's house for Thanksgiving, an American family festival.

◀ Mum wants to make this photo into a Christmas card.

Activity

Using a scrap book and some glue, make your own family photo album. Try to include as many relatives as you can. Ask older people in your family to help you. They may have photos of distant cousins you have never even heard of!

◀ Our house is built on stilts. It is made of timber and bamboo. This is me sitting on the top of the ladder with my dad and little sister.

Rudy

My name is Rudy. I live in Borneo. My dad, mum, sister and I live with about thirty other families in a long wooden house on stilts. Each family has its own special part of the house for cooking and sleeping. It sometimes gets a bit noisy, but there are always enough children for a game of football!

9

Our Homes

The building we live in is our home. It is a place where a family can be together to eat, sleep, relax and play. There are all kinds of different homes around the world. Some people live in tall blocks of flats, while others live in small houses or huts. Our homes are built to suit the weather of the country we live in.

▲ This house in southern Africa is made of clay. It has been decorated with patterns. A family of six people lives here.

▶ Many families live in this huge block of flats in Bombay, India. From the top you can see for miles over the city. The walls and floors are made of concrete, held up by a skeleton of steel girders.

Look Closer

Some people live in homes that float. These houseboats are on the River Thames in London. Houseboats do not have gardens, so people sometimes put pots of flowers on the roof. On a houseboat you need to be friendly with your neighbours, because you may have to climb across their boats to get to your front door!

◀ This stone house is in Edinburgh, Scotland. It used to be a house for one family, but today it is divided into three flats.

▶ This Russian house is made from logs, cut from the forest around it. In the winter, the family spend most of their time around a big stove in the kitchen.

Oyun

My name is Oyun. I live in Mongolia. My home is a big, round tent called a ger. It has a wooden frame, covered with felt and canvas. Inside, my home is warm and colourful. It is full of painted furniture and brightly coloured rugs. The ger has one large room where we eat, sleep, play and do our homework. If my brother gets really annoying, I just go out for a ride on my pony.

▲ A ger can be moved easily. This is a family putting up their ger.

▶ This is my brother and me having tea with my mum.

Town and Country

Our homes are usually grouped together in villages, towns or cities. Children who live in the country may have forests or fields to play in. Children in towns and cities play in gardens, streets or parks. Villages do not usually have many shops, so people may have to travel to towns to buy things. People in large towns and cities have most things they need nearby.

▲ This the kraal. In the day, families eat, work and play here.

Moses's village

Moses lives in a village in southern Africa. It has no shops and is a long way from the nearest town. The villagers grow or make most of the things they need. Moses's mum makes cooking pots and cloth for clothes. His dad built their house and looks after it. The houses in the village are built around a space called the 'kraal'. At night, the villagers herd their animals into the kraal to keep them safe.

Ines's village

Ines lives in a village in Spain. The biggest building there is the church, which is right in the centre. The square outside the church is a meeting place. Ines plays here with her friends after school. There is a doctor, a baker, a small supermarket and a cafe, but no school in the village. Ines catches a bus every day to the school in a nearby town.

▶ The village square. In the summer everyone gathers for a party here.

◀ Some villages grow bigger and become towns. Seaside towns often grow up in places where there is a beach and a good harbour for boats. This is Brighton, a seaside town in England. In the summer lots of tourists visit, and on hot days the beaches are really crowded. In winter many of the shops, cafes and restaurants close, and the town feels empty.

Kristin and Mario

Activity

Write a leaflet full of information for children moving into your area. Try to think of things other children would like to know. Where are the best places to play? Which is the best sweet shop or tree to climb? You could illustrate your leaflet with pictures, photos and maps.

▲ This is our village.

Kristin

I'm Kristin. I live in a village in the mountains in Norway. The mountains look very beautiful all covered in snow. My village is very small, and sometimes I wish there were more shops and a cinema. My parents say that years ago many more families lived here, but most of them moved to towns. In the winter, I ski every day.

▶ This is me with my dog, Roald.

▲ The market is a fun place to meet my friends. Sometimes we get food from a stall and sit and eat it in the market square.

Mario

My name is Mario. I live in a town in the mountains in Guatemala. Most days it is quiet, but on market days the town is packed. People set up stalls selling fruit and vegetables, clothes, pots – all sorts of things. I earn money by running errands for them.

▶ This is me wearing my favourite boots.

15

Cities

Big cities are some of the most exciting places in the world, where millions of people live, work and play together. Today, more and more people in the world are moving from the countryside into cities.

By night

Cities never seem to sleep. At night, they are alive with people out having fun. Cinemas, theatres, nightclubs, bars and restaurants all stay open until late. Some streets are more crowded at night than they are in the day!

▲ In many parts of a city it never gets dark, because the streets are lit up with multi-coloured lights.

▼ This is a big Japanese city at night.

By day

By day, too, cities are bustling with activity. Thousands of workers, shoppers and tourists fill the streets. People eat and drink in restaurants and cafes, and children play in the parks.

Having so many people in one place does cause problems. Many streets are clogged with cars and lorries. The fumes from this traffic make the air dirty, and can make people ill. Some cities have streets where no traffic is allowed.

◀ Only people are allowed on this city street in Stockholm. This makes being in the area less dangerous, less crowded and less smelly.

Look Closer

Some cities, such as Rome, the capital of Italy, have a long history. Modern office blocks, stores and roads exist next to ancient buildings, some of which are more than a thousand years old.

▲ This building is the Coliseum in Rome. The ancient Romans built it nearly 2000 years ago. They used to watch gladiators fight here.

Taylor and Budi

Taylor

My name is Taylor. I live in San Francisco, in the United States. Our house is in a suburb on the edge of the city. My mum and dad drive into the city every day to work, but I hardly ever go. I don't really need to, because there are shops, a school, a cinema, a park and a swimming pool, all near my home.

▲ My house has a big garden and a garage.

▼ This is me in our neighbour's garden. I'm the one in the pink bikini. We love playing around with the water sprinkler.

▲ This is me playing with my friends. We play in the street because we have no garden. I'm the one in the T-shirt with the striped sleeves.

Budi

My name is Budi. I live in Jakarta, the capital of Indonesia. I live in a house made of corrugated iron right next to this canal. The canal is very dirty. It is full of rubbish and the water smells. In the summer, it is very hot in Jakarta. I wish the water was cleaner so I could go swimming to cool off, but Mum says the water would make me ill.

Activity

Wherever we live in the world, we must look after our water and not waste it. There are some simple things you can do to save water, such as not keeping the tap running when you are cleaning your teeth and collecting rainwater to water the garden. Can you think of any other ways to save water?

Farming

Most of the food we eat comes from farms. The crops farmers grow and the animals they keep are affected by the weather and the soil. For example, the Arctic wouldn't be a very good place to grow bananas! But it's not only food that comes from farms. Farmers also grow crops such as cotton, and keep sheep for their wool.

Herding

Some farmers who keep animals move them from place to place, to find fresh water and food. This is called 'herding'. Herders in Kenya live in simple homes made out of thorn bushes, mud and animal dung, because they know they will soon be on the move again. Each time they move, they build new homes.

◀ This Kenyan woman is herding goats. The kid she is carrying may have lost its mother.

▶ At harvest time, huge combine harvesters cut the wheat and separate the grain from the rest of the plant.

Rice farms

More than half the people in the world eat rice every day, so rice farming is very important. This rice farm is on an island called Bali, in Indonesia. The rice is grown in fields called 'paddies'. The paddies are in steps up the hillside. In the rainy season the paddies are flooded. Strong stone walls stop the water and soil from washing away down the hill.

◀ This rice farmer is checking his fields for weeds.

Look Closer

Every year about 80 million tonnes of fish are caught in the world's seas and oceans. Some fishermen catch just enough fish for themselves and their families. But in some countries, fishing is big business.

▲ Japanese fishing boats are floating fish factories. Their huge nets catch many tonnes of fish. Below decks, the fish are cleaned and then frozen. This keeps them fresh on long voyages.

Intensive farms

Intensive farmers use high-tech machines and chemicals to get as much as they possibly can from their land. This intensive farm is in the Ukraine. The fields of wheat are enormous, to make it easier for large machines to work in them. The machines can do the work of many workers in a much shorter time.

Hugh, Adanna and Daniel

Hugh

I live on a really big sheep-station in Australia. We have nearly 3,000 sheep. Our nearest neighbours live about two hours' drive away. It's too far to go to the nearest school, so Mum teaches me at home. If I need help with my lessons, there are teachers I can talk to on a two-way radio. I love living on the station, but sometimes I wish I could see more of my friends.

▼ This is me and Greg, my older brother, feeding some lambs. If any of the lambs are sick Mum looks after them in the house.

Adanna

I live on a small farm in Nigeria. We have a few cows and goats and grow corn, potatoes, vegetables and bananas. If we grow more than we can eat, we sell what's left over at the local market. All my family have to work really hard on the farm. We don't have a tractor, so all the work is done by hand.

▶ Mum is teaching me how to milk our goat, so I can do the milking before I go to school. I love the sound the milk makes as it squirts into the bucket.

Daniel

I live on a coffee plantation in Tanzania. Our coffee beans are sold all over the world. Harvest is our busiest time of year. I stay at home to help instead of going to school. First we pick the coffee cherries from the bushes. Then we mush them up, wash them, and dry them until only the bean in the middle is left.

◀ This is me with my brothers and cousins checking the beans before they are sold. I am wearing a white T-shirt.

Making Things

People all over the world make things for others to buy. Some things are made at home and are sold in local shops or markets. Other things are made in enormous factories and sold all over the world.

◀ This rubber duck was made in China, but was sold in a shop in Sweden.

Workers of the world

Some workers are craftspeople. They use their hands to make beautiful objects such as wooden animals, rugs or pots. Many traditional craft skills have been passed on from parents to children for hundreds of years. Other workers may operate a machine which makes just one tiny part of a complicated product such as an aeroplane or a car. These workers may never see the finished product they have helped to make.

▶ Umbrella-makers know their product will never go out of fashion. As long as there are rainy places in the world people will need umbrellas to keep dry.

◀ In modern factories such as this car plant, robots are used instead of people.

▲ This is me in the workshop (I am in the middle). Of all the things we make, I like the peacocks best.

Activity

Big companies spend millions of pounds advertising the things they make, to try to persuade people to buy them. Try designing an advertising poster yourself, for one of your favourite toys. Make the poster bright and eye-catching. Think about what it is about that toy that makes it special.

It's COOL! It's FAB! It's...
Manic Mouse
The _ultimate_ computer game
Can you save Manic Mouse from Crazy Cat?

Padma

My name is Padma. I work in a small workshop in India, making metal ornaments. I work there with my father and brothers, after school and in the holidays. We sell our ornaments in the market. Many are bought by tourists who want to take home something beautiful from India.

Yusta

My name is Yusta. I live on the island of Zanzibar, off the coast of Africa. I am weaving a makawa, a cone-shaped food cover made of straw. We use makawas to keep the sun and the flies off our food. I am making a new makawa for my family and some to sell to other families. My father says I am the best weaver in my village.

▶ My brother and sisters like to watch me weave. They will learn too, when they are older.

25

Shopping

Most people can't grow or make everything they need, so they have to buy things from shops. Some shops are enormous and sell lots of different things. Others are tiny and sell just one sort of thing, such as cheese. What sort of shops do you like going to?

Kelvin

My name is Kelvin. Every week Mum and I go to the supermarket. I help her push the trolley when it gets full and heavy. Mum and I don't always agree about what we should buy. I like cereals covered with honey and sugar, but mum says they will ruin my teeth. If I make enough fuss, I usually get my own way!

▲ Each of these Chinese women is a shopkeeper. They are all selling petrol from roadside stalls.

▼ This cereal packet has got my favourite cartoon character on it.

▲ The spices are beautiful colours.

Ravi

My name is Ravi. My dad has a spice stall at a bazaar (market) in Calcutta, India. The spices are ground into powder and heaped into dishes. Most Indians use spices in their cooking, so lots of people come to our stall. Once, when I was helping dad, I sneezed and coloured powders blew all over the counter! Dad was not pleased. I ran away and hid in the bazaar until he had calmed down.

Activity

Imagine it is a special occasion and you have to buy a present for everyone in your family. Write a shopping list. How many shops would you have to visit to buy all the things on your list?

Shopping list

mum	flowers
dad	screwdriver set
gran	chocs
Tom	yoyo
Susie	crayons

Favourite Foods

We all need to eat to stay alive. But cooking and eating can also be good fun. People in different parts of the world enjoy different kinds of food. These children tell you about what they like to eat best.

Nok

My name is Nok. I live in Thailand. I love all the delicious fruits that grow in my country, but my favourites are melons. They are sweet and very, very juicy. I buy melons from a fruit stall at the side of the road.

Sergei

My name is Sergei. I live in Russia. My favourite food is ice cream. Every year we go to an ice cream parlour for my birthday. I like mint choc chip flavour the best.

Antonio

My name is Antonio. I am Italian and I love pizza. My favourite pizza topping is cheese, tomato and pepperoni. Every Saturday my dad and I make pizzas for lunch.

Jordan

My name is Jordan. I live in Kenya. My favourite food is chicken stew with yams. Nearly all the ingredients for this dish come from my family's farm because we keep chickens and grow yams in our vegetable garden. This is me digging the yams out of the ground.

Activity

Not all the food you eat comes from your own country. Some of it may come from the other side of the world! Look at the food in your store cupboard or fridge. The labels will tell you where the food came from. Look at a world map to find out which food has travelled farthest.

Working for Others

Many people have jobs doing things for others. Think about how many people have jobs doing things for you. Teachers, dentists, shop assistants and children's TV presenters are just a few. Here are some jobs people do for us.

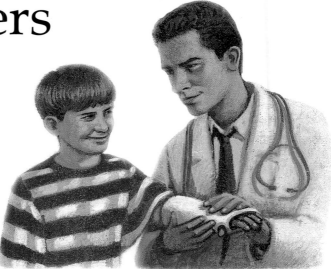

▲ Doctors and nurses look after us when we are ill or hurt. This boy has broken his arm falling out of a tree. The doctor is putting it in plaster.

◀ Artists and performers entertain us, and sometimes surprise us! These performers are doing a show for people in the street.

Look Closer

Many jobs that used to be done by people are now done by machines or computers. For example, you can get money from a cash machine in the street, instead of from a person in a bank.

▼ If a building catches fire, firefighters soon arrive to put the fire out. They use axes and crowbars to get into the building, and breathing masks to keep out the smoky air.

▲ Bus drivers take us from place to place. This bus in Pakistan has been decorated with fabulous colours and pictures. It is crowded with people going to the local market town.

▼ Police officers help to keep us safe. They try to make sure people don't break the law, and they catch people who do.

Children at School

Do you go to school? Most children do. But schools are different in different parts of the world. The subjects you learn, the times you go to school, even the school buildings, all depend on where you live.

▶ This is me at school. I am sitting next to my sister Rupati, the girl with the bright pink bow in her hair. We often have lessons outside because it is so warm.

Abdul

My name is Abdul. I live in Bangladesh. We are very lucky that there is a school in our village: many villages don't have one. There are 60 children in my school, but only one teacher. We learn reading, writing and maths, as well as lessons about farming and health. School starts really early, before it gets too hot. Lessons stop at lunchtime, and in the afternoons we work on our parents' farms.

I am the only one in my family who can read. I help my parents by reading for them. I feel very proud that I can be useful.

Activity

Write a letter to Abdul or Anna telling them about your school day. Tell them what you like about their school, and what you would find strange. Do you think they would enjoy going to your school?

32

Anna

My name is Anna. I live in the USA. I catch a yellow bus to school every morning. Most days we do reading, writing and maths, but we also have singing, art, P.E., geography and history.

My favourite lesson is art. At 11.30 I eat my packed lunch, then we have more lessons until 2.30, when we go home. After school I like to watch television, or play with my brother.

◀ Here I am at school. I'm sitting next to the teacher.

Look Closer

Like Abdul and his sister, many children all over the world have to work to help their parents. This often means they have to miss school.

▼ This Moroccan boy is hard at work decorating objects made out of leather.

▲ Fetching water is an important job, but it can be a long walk to the nearest pump. This boy in Guinea has been sent by his mum to collect water.

Children at Play

When school's over and you've finished your homework, what do you like to do best? From listening to music to going to the zoo, there are lots of fun things to do and see in your free time. These children tell you about the things they enjoy doing most.

Jacques

My name is Jacques and I love playing football. I live in a city called Port au Prince in Haiti. There are no football pitches near my home, so I play in the streets. I play every day after school with my friends until it gets too dark to see the ball. One day I would like to have my own pair of football boots with proper studs.

▶ This is me playing football with my friend Bertrand. I am the one in bare feet.

Miguel

My name is Miguel, and I live in Mexico. My sisters and I love to watch game shows on TV. Most of the programmes are made in the USA and dubbed into Spanish. You can tell, because people's words never match up with the way their mouths move.

◀ Our house only has one room, so some of us sit on the bed to watch the TV.

Look Closer

These days, many families go abroad for their holidays. This means children from different countries can get to know each other. This is a postcard from Boris, who is on holiday in Morocco.

Dear Stefan
Having a great time. Made a Moroccan friend called Ayoub. He does cartwheels. Ayoub's house has a flat roof. He sleeps there when it is very hot. The food here is quite spicy. Ayoub likes it, but I don't!
Love Boris

▶ Do you like playing around in water? Most children do. Wherever you go, swimming, diving and splashing are good exercise and great fun. Some swimming pools have enormous water slides, called flumes, which whoosh you down into the pool.

William

My name is William. I live in the UK. My favourite outing is a trip to the fair that comes to my town every summer. I like a ride called Death Slide the best. It is really scary. I feel sick and dizzy when I get off, but I don't mind. Last year Dad won a gigantic pink teddy at the coconut shy.

▼ This is me in front of the chair ride, wearing my Arsenal football shirt.

What We Believe

Many people in the world have religious beliefs. Most religions teach that there is an invisible power beyond our everyday lives. This power is often given a name – a God or gods. Religions usually have rules and beliefs about what is right and wrong, why we are born and what happens when we die.

Christianity

Christians follow the teachings of Jesus Christ, who lived about 2000 years ago. They believe that Jesus was God's son. Their holy book is the Bible. It tells how Jesus came to Earth, was put to death on a cross and three days later came alive again, before returning to be with God in heaven. Jesus taught that God is loving and always ready to forgive people. On Sundays, many Christians worship together in a church.

▲ My name is Sophie. At Christmas my school puts on a nativity play which tells the story of how Jesus was born in a stable. This is me being Mary, Jesus's mother. It is the most important part in the play.

Judaism

Jewish people believe that there is one God. They believe that, thousands of years ago, God made an agreement with the Jews that they would be his chosen people. In return, they promised to keep God's laws. These laws are written down in a holy book called the Torah. From Friday evening to Saturday evening is a special day of rest and prayer called Shabbat.

◀ Hanukkah is a Jewish festival. Every day, for eight days, children light a new candle on the Hanukkah candlestick.

Islam

▼ My name is Mahmood. On Fridays, I go to the mosque with my dad and brothers to say my prayers. Before I go in, I have to wash myself and take off my shoes. This is me in the mosque. I am sitting on the floor, waiting for prayers to begin.

People who follow the Islamic religion are called Muslims. Like Jews and Christians, Muslims believe in one God, who they call Allah. They believe Allah spoke to people on earth through the Prophet Muhammad, a man who lived in Arabia 1300 years ago. Allah's words were written down in a holy book called the Qur'an. Muslim children are taught to read and recite the Qur'an.

◀ My name is Lobsang. I am 10 years old. I live in a Buddhist temple, where I am studying to become a monk. If I decide I don't want to be a monk, I will go back and live with my family.

▲ The temple where I live is in Tibet, China.

Buddhism

Buddhists do not have any god. They follow the teachings of Buddha, who lived about 2,500 years ago. Buddha travelled the country teaching that pain and suffering are caused by selfishness. Buddhists must try to be kind in all they think, say and do. Meditating helps them to do this. They sit quietly and try to fill their minds with holy thoughts.

Hinduism

Hindus worship many gods. They believe that when a person dies he or she will be born again in another body. People who are good will be reborn into a better life than before. But someone who has hurt others may be born into a more difficult life. Hindus worship at a shrine in their home, and may also go to a temple. Hinduism is the main religion in India.

▶ My name is Sanjay. I live in north-west India. Holi is a Hindu springtime festival. We throw brightly coloured powder at each other and squirt each other with water. This is me and my cousins with our bottles of water. I'm the small one in the middle.

Other religions

There are many other religions in the world. Some have millions of followers, but others have only a few hundred. Sikhs believe in one God. They believe that God is in all things and that all people are equal. Sikh temples are called gurdwaras. Their holy book, the Guru Granth Sahib, is kept on a throne in the gurdwara. Taoism is a Chinese religion. Taoists believe in many gods and try to live in harmony with nature.

▼ My name is Yoko. My family follows the Shinto religion. We believe that there are many gods in nature, in animals and in people – even the dead. In this photo I am visiting a holy place called a shrine, to ask the gods to help me with my exams.

Let's Celebrate!

All over the world people enjoy special occasions when they can dress up, eat special food, sing, dance and have a party. The occasion might be a birthday, a celebration of nature or a religious festival. These children tell you about their favourite celebrations.

▲ Here I am in my carnival outfit. I love the procession and the dancing!

Maria

My name is Maria. I live in Rio de Janeiro in Brazil. My favourite celebration is the carnival that takes place in my city every year. The carnival used to be the last chance for a feast before Lent, a time when Christians were not supposed to eat meat. Today thousands of dancers parade through the streets dressed up in spectacular costumes. It is very noisy and exciting.

Activity

Make a piñata, a decorated ball stuffed full of sweets. On birthdays in Mexico, a piñata is hung up, and children break it open with sticks. To make this piñata fish, first cover a balloon with papier mâché. Once the papier mâché is dry, pop the balloon, then cut a mouth at the big end. Add a tail and fins made from cardboard, and glue on a piece of string to hang it from. Now paint the piñata in bright colours, and fill it with sweets!

Hallowe'en

In the USA, Hallowe'en, on 31st October, is a fun festival. It dates back to a time when people believed the spirits of the dead could be seen on that night. People dress up as witches and make lanterns out of pumpkins.

▲ With their carved faces and candles inside, the lanterns look very spooky!

▼ In China, the new year is a big celebration. On the streets of Beijing there are firecrackers, and a beautiful paper dragon is carried through the streets.

Helena

My name is Helena. I live in Sweden. My favourite celebration is the feast day of Santa Lucia on 13th December, when we girls dress up in white robes and wear crowns of candles on our heads. We walk slowly through the streets, singing carols. After the procession we eat buns called 'lussekatts', made with saffron and raisins.

► Here I am dressed up as Santa Lucia. She is the patron saint of light.

Our Future

Everyone has dreams for the future. In poorer parts of the world, children want to be sure they will have enough food to eat and clean water to drink. Here some of the children from the book tell you about their ambitions.

Lobsang

I think I would like to stay at my temple for the rest of my life and become a proper Buddhist monk. I would miss my family, but everyone is very kind here and I have everything I need. Maybe one day, if I studied and meditated hard, I would be wise enough to be the abbot (head) of our temple.

Sophie

I enjoyed doing my nativity play at school so much, I would like to be an actress. When I am older, I will have to go to a special acting school. I would like to act in films and be a rich and famous movie star. I will probably go and live in Hollywood, in a big house with a swimming pool.

Hugh

When I grow up I would like to be a flying doctor. Flying doctors are very important in Australia. They fly in planes to visit patients who live in places where there are no hospitals or surgeries. A flying doctor saved my brother's life when his appendix burst. I know I will have to study hard and pass lots of exams before I can be a doctor.

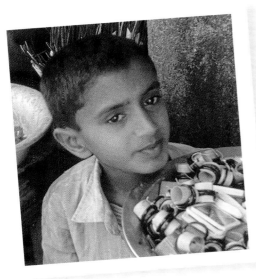

Ravi

When I'm older, I want to work in the bazaar like dad, but I'd like to sell beautiful jewellery instead of spices. Maybe one day I will have my own shop, and sell gold and silver bracelets to the rich ladies of Calcutta.

Ayce

When I grow up I would like to help make the world a cleaner place. I think it is very important that we protect our world and stop people from polluting the rivers and seas. I think it is very sad that some animals may soon be extinct. I want to stop that from happening.

43

Fact File

Africa

Africa

Kenya

Capital city: Nairobi
Main religions: Christian, traditional African beliefs

Kenya is in East Africa. On the coast it is hot and rainy, but inland it is much drier. In the mountains, farmers grow crops such as tea and coffee. Tourists visit the great grasslands of Kenya, which are home to many wild animals.

Nigeria

Capital city: Abuja
Main religions: Muslim, Christian, traditional African religions

Nigeria is in West Africa. More people live here than in any other African country. Nigeria could be a very rich country because it has good farmland and oil. But bad governments and wars have kept the people poor.

South Africa

Capital city: Cape Town, Pretoria, Bloemfontein
Main religions: Christian, traditional African religions

South Africa is the richest country in Africa. It has mountains, fertile valleys, grasslands and beautiful coastlines. Until 1994, only the white settlers in South Africa could vote, but today it is a proper democracy.

Tanzania

Capital city: Dodoma
Main religions: Christian, Muslim, traditional African religions

Tanzania became a country when the old country of Tanganyika joined together with Zanzibar, an island in the Indian Ocean. It has a beautiful coast lined with coral reefs. Inland, the flat grassy plains of the Serengeti have been turned into one of the most famous nature reserves in the world.

Australasia

Australasia

Australia

Capital city: Canberra
Main religion: Christian

Australia is a large country in the South Pacific Ocean. Most Australians live by the coast, because the middle of the country (the outback) is very hot and dry. Aboriginal people have lived in Australia for thousands of years, but in the last 200 years people from Europe and Asia have come to live here.

North and South America

Brazil

Capital city: Brasilia
Main religion: Christian

Brazil is the biggest country in South America. It contains the largest rainforest in the world. Brazil used to belong to Portugal, so the people in Brazil speak Portuguese. Most Brazilians live in crowded cities near the coast.

Canada

Capital city: Ottawa
Main religion: Christian

Canada is the second largest country in the world, but most of it is too cold or mountainous for people. Three-quarters of all Canadians live in cities in the south. Canada has two official languages: English and French.

Guatemala

Capital city: Guatemala City
Main religion: Christian

Guatemala is in Central America. Most people are farmers growing coffee, bananas, cotton, sugar and rice. Guatemala suffers many earthquakes, volcanoes and hurricanes.

North and South America

Haiti

Capital city: Port au Prince
Main religion: Christian, voodoo

Haiti is an island country in the warm Caribbean Sea. Most Haitians are farmers, but the land is not good for farming. Haitians speak their own version of French, called French Creole.

United States of America (USA)

Capital city: Washington DC
Main religion: Christian

The USA is the world's richest and most powerful country. American products, from cola drinks to computers, sell all over the world. Nearly all Americans are descended from settlers who have come to live here in the past 400 years. Most people live in large cities on the coasts.

Asia

Bangladesh

Capital city: Dhaka
Main religions: Muslim, Hindu

Bangladesh is a flat, marshy country. It is one of the most crowded countries in the world. Most of the people there are farmers. Every year during the rainy season (from June to October) the three big rivers in Bangladesh flood. Many people lose their homes, animals and crops.

Asia

China
Capital city: Beijing
Main religion: None

China is a vast country. It is almost the same size as the whole of Europe, and there are more people than in any other country. China contains many different kinds of countryside and climate, from snow-topped mountains to tropical islands.

India
Capital city: New Delhi
Main religions: Hindu, Muslim

India is a very large country in Asia. Nearly a billion people live there. Most Indians still live in villages and farm the land. Summers are very hot, but between June and September the monsoon wind brings welcome rain to much of the country.

Indonesia
Capital city: Jakarta
Main religion: Muslim

Indonesia is made up of 13,677 islands, but over half of all Indonesians live on just one island – Java. The weather is hot and wet. This is good for farmers to grow rice, which is the country's basic food.

Mongolia
Capital city: Ulan Bator
Main religion: None

Mongolia is in central Asia. Many Mongolians live on grassy plains in the middle of the country, where they herd animals. Mongolia has short, hot summers and long, cold winters.

Russia
Capital city: Moscow
Main religion: Christian

Russia is the biggest country in the world. Most people live in the west of Russia where the farmland is better and the weather is warmer. In the east is Siberia – a vast, cold land where only a few people live.

Saudi Arabia
Capital city: Riyadh
Main religion: Muslim

Saudi Arabia is mainly desert. There is some farmland in the middle of the country, but there is so little rain that it is difficult to grow crops. The Muslim prophet Mohammed was born in Saudi Arabia. The country is very rich because it sells lots of oil.

Thailand
Capital city: Bangkok
Main religion: Buddhist

Thailand is a tropical country in South-east Asia. For most of the year it is hot and sticky, and there is a lot of rain. This makes it ideal for growing rice. Thailand sells more rice abroad than any other country in the world.

Turkey
Capital city: Ankara
Main religion: Muslim

Most of Turkey is in Asia, but its western tip is in Europe. The centre of Turkey is an area of flat, high ground where the land is good for farming. Lots of tourists visit the beaches of southern Turkey.

Europe

Italy
Capital city: Rome
Main religion: Christian

Italy is a country in southern Europe. In the north there are many busy cities and big factories, but in the south most people are farmers. Lots of tourists come to visit Italy for its beautiful old buildings and paintings.

Norway
Capital city: Oslo
Main religion: Christian

Norway is a country in northern Europe. The north of Norway is in the freezing Arctic. Much of the land is mountains covered with forests, so there aren't many farms. Lots of people in Norway work in fishing.

Spain
Capital city: Madrid
Main religion: Christian

Spain is a big country in south-west Europe. Much of it is a huge treeless plain, where the summers are scorching and the winters freezing. Many tourists come to southern Spain to enjoy its hot summers and sandy beaches.

Europe

Sweden
Capital city: Stockholm
Main religion: Christian

Sweden is a country in northern Europe. The northern part is in the Arctic, but the south is warmer and the land better for farming. In the middle of the country there are many factories, making goods such as cars and computers.

United Kingdom (UK)
Capital city: London
Main religion: Christian
The UK is made up of England, Scotland, Wales and Northern Ireland. The countryside ranges from mountains to flat marshy lands. Most people in the UK live in cities or towns.

Index

Acknowledgements

Artwork

Pages 6–7 Martin Sanders; 9bl Stephen Gulbis; 10tl, tr, 11tl, tr, bl Julian Baker; 12, 13t Mark Edwards; 14tr Stephen Gulbis; 19br Stephen Gulbis; 21cr Mark Edwards; 25tr Stephen Gulbis; 28, 29l, tr Mark Edwards; 29br Stephen Gulbis; 30–31 Mark Edwards; 36bl Ellen Beier; 40b, 40–41 Stephen Gulbis; 42t, br, 43t, cl, br Mark Edwards.

Photos

The publishers would like to thank the following for permission to reproduce photographs.

Page 6t B. Toutee/Colorific!; 6b Explorer/Robert Harding Picture Library; 7t A. Woolfitt/Robert Harding Picture Library; 7b J. Horner/Corbis; 8l J. Blair/Corbis; 8r B. Erlanson/The Image Bank; 9 D. Maybury/Eye Ubiquitous/Corbis; 10 T. Dosogne/The Image Bank; 11 T. Nebbia/Corbis; 13 R. Rainford/Robert Harding Picture Library; 14 P. Hermansen/NHPA; 14t (inset) Hermansen/NHPA; 14b (inset) A. Woolfitt/Robert Harding Picture Library; 15t B. Kennedy/Planet Earth Pictures; 15b Robert Harding/Explorer; 16 inset T. Bean/Corbis; 16 M. Stephenson/Corbis; 17t N. Wheeler/Corbis; 17b M. Beebe/Corbis; 18t C. Zobel/Corbis; 18b S. Justice/ The Image Bank; 19 D. Lamont/Corbis; 20–21 M.S. Yamashita/Corbis; 20 T. Magor/ Robert Harding Picture Library; 21 D. Conger/Corbis; 22 P. Tweedie/Corbis; 23t D. Harcourt Webster/Robert Harding Picture Library; 23b Photri Inc./Robert Harding Picture Library; p24l S. Rowell/Telegraph Colour Library; 25t T. Gervis/Robert Harding Picture Library; 25br D.G. Houser/Corbis; 26t K. R. Morris/Corbis; 26b L. Dwight/Corbis; 27 J. Horner/Corbis; 32 Sean Sprague/UNICEF/CF45-2; 33bl M. Murray-Lee/UNICEF; 33br John Isaac/UNICEF/87-018/Morocco; 34t P.A. Souders/Corbis; 34b Hanel/V. Thomas/Telegraph Colour Library; 35t J. Sugar/Corbis; 35b C. Bowman/Robert Harding Picture Library; 36 S. Bavister/Robert Harding Picture Library; 37 M.S. Yamashita/Corbis; 38t J. Horner/Corbis; 38b Telegraph Colour Library; 39t H. Rogers/Trip; 39b M.S. Yamashita/ Corbis; 40t B. Toutee/Colorific!; 41t J. Corwin/Tony Stone Images; 41b Explorer/Robert Harding Picture Library.